Colors
for
Living

Living Rooms

BY MELINDA LEVINE
PRINCIPAL PHOTOGRAPHERS: RUSSELL ABRAHAM AND KENNETH RICE

ROCKPORT

Dedication

To the colorful Ken and Mo:
Thanks for your abounding patience with a
project that kept getting bigger.

First published in the United States of America by:
Rockport Publishers, Inc.
33 Commercial Street
Gloucester, MA 01930
Telephone: (978) 282-9590
Fax: (978) 283-2742

ISBN 1-56496-553-8

2 4 6 8 10 9 7 5 3 1

Production: Sara Day Graphic Design
Cover Photograph: Tim Street-Porter

Printed in Hong Kong

Colors

for

Living

Living Rooms

GLOUCESTER MASSACHUSETTS

ROCKPORT PUBLISHERS

TABLE OF CONTENTS

Photo: Kenneth Rice
Design: Agnes Bourne

INTRODUCTION

The success of your living room depends on the strength of its parts—color, architecture, furnishings, surface treatments—and how they complement one another. A well-coordinated combination of disparate elements—shape of space, proportions, lighting, forms, textures, function, and color—will virtually guarantee good design and a living room made for living. This book is dedicated to the single most important and influential of these elements: color.

In any living room, there are three basic areas of color: the walls and floors, the upholstery and window coverings, and the accents: art, pillows, and accessories. If one of these color areas is out of balance, it will upset the design and ambience of the entire room. Even the same two colors can create strikingly different effects when used in different proportions. For example, the calm atmosphere of a room that is predominantly gray green and has chief accents in turquoise would take on an entirely different mood if the color ratio were reversed: a turquoise room with flashes of gray green.

There are no hard-and-fast rules about color. Although certain colors are rarely seen together in living rooms, almost any color will work in combination with any other color if hue, tone, and tint are balanced. And today, color choices are more varied than ever. Bold, adventurous colors are right at home in the living room; so are pale, weathered naturals—

and every color in between. Wall treatments are rich and layered; color is no longer just painted on but, rather, is built up. The resulting finish is a rich, deep, and complex patina, often revealing—as parchment or marble would—a range of shades within.

HOW TO USE THIS BOOK

Although most of the rooms illustrated in this book were designed by professionals, you, too, can design the living room of your dreams. Use this book as a source for ideas that work. Select the color schemes that you like—a palette accompanies each photograph—and start your plan there. Color is the first building block. Once that is in place, other design decisions become less intimidating, even enjoyable!

The color samples in the back of the book represent the individual palettes arranged in color-wheel, or rainbow, order. Browse through these, and when you find a color that you like, turn to the page listed for an example of a palette using that color.

Before you choose your colors, consider the mood you want for your room: tranquil, restful, joyous, romantic, or energetic. In the first chapter, read about mood and color—nothing will affect mood as much as color will—then visit the interiors that follow, and begin to think about your color choices. It is that easy. What are you waiting for?

A limited palette—white, black, and soaring red—creates a distinctive space.

COLOR AND LIVING

Color is a magician. It can instantly transform a living room from a plain beige box to a glowing green-blue jewel, from a nondescript white room to a sunny yellow and violet sanctuary, from an everyday gray cube to a distinctive space of white, black, and soaring red. Color can alter the appearance of space—it can push away walls or bring them forward. Color can make a small room seem larger; a dark room, lighter. Color can impart a range of moods, from cool and aloof to warm and intimate. A flick of a paint-laden brush, the placement of a vivid carpet, or a toss of some brilliant silk pillows, can instantly change the atmosphere of a room, like magic.

Color can emphasize architectural features or cover them up. Here, the deep teal accentuates the geometry of the fireplace mantel.

THE MOOD OF A ROOM

Color is powerful, but, ultimately, our subjective response to a certain color is what determines its real impact. Color can make us feel excited, happy, nervous, soothed, or sad. Some people feel closed in by a living room with maroon or navy walls and overwhelmed by so much color intensity. But to others, those deeply colored walls seem friendly and comforting. Most people find off-white, beige, and pale green restful and pleasant. Yet some find that a room with these colors is too calm, even boring, unless it is perked up by brilliant accents.

Certain colors can influence mood somewhat predictably. Red is an exciting color; red walls, carpets, or prominent accessories are often used in restaurants to stimulate diners' appetites. Yellow is cheerful; like a sunny day, it makes us feel good. Blue, the color of the ocean and sky, is tranquil, but too much can be depressing. Green is refreshing, like a summer walk in a forest. We make babies' rooms feel soft and soothing with pastels of pink, blue, green, and yellow. Few parents would risk using hot pink, wild zebra stripes, or red with electric blue trim for the nursery walls. But in a living room, bold color schemes can work. Deciding on the mood you want to convey is the first step in the decorating process.

THE SHAPE OF COLOR

Color can change the apparent shape of space, emphasize or cover up architecture, complement proportions, and enhance or reduce the energy of a room. Dark colors make a wall recede, and light colors bring it forward. Wall and ceiling color can accentuate beautiful architectural details such as lintels, scroll friezes, bas-reliefs, exposed beams, and wainscoting. Contrasting colors can dramatically emphasize carved moldings or trim. Color can also downplay the faults of a room: lumpy walls, boring cubelike shapes, low ceilings, less-than-seamless renovations. Nothing compensates for the imperfections of a wall as well as a rich, deep coat of paint.

Conventional wisdom says that if you have a tiny room, you have to paint it white or a very pale tint to make it appear larger. Yet light wall tints should be used with care. They certainly make a room look more spacious and airy, but the result can be monotonous unless darker shades and contrasting colors are worked into the scheme. But, if we decide to fly in the face of convention and paint that tiny, boring white cube a brilliant aquamarine, suddenly we have a glowing jewel of a space. Although the actual square footage of the room did not grow one inch, the color choice has creatively compensated for the deficiency of the room.

Subtly contrasting colors bring out the detailed patterns of the ceiling in this room.

PATTERN AND TEXTURE

You can add color to a room by the walls, furnishings, floor and window treatments, and accessories, using solid colors or patterns. In interior design, mixing patterns has moved in and out of favor over the centuries, and today it has become fashionable again. Contemporary living rooms, even those with traditional decor, use contrasting patterns in abundance. It is a busy, eclectic look, but one that is also warm and inviting. The secret to the success of matching patterns is that they must be related in some way. For example, each pattern in the motif shares a color—perhaps a theme of coral running through all the prints—or a similar repeating shape.

In more exotic-looking living rooms, especially those featuring ethnic elements and folk art, there is a compelling mix of bold and subtle pattern, texture, and color: handwoven and knotted kilims; African mudcloth pillows, drapes, or upholstery; deeply etched and patterned brass tables from India; Mexican or African masks; vibrant batiked Indonesian cloths; brightly painted and detailed Oaxacan wood animals; and Japanese ikat pillows and throws. The possibilities of pattern and color combinations are as broad as the globe itself.

Too bold a pattern on the walls limits the number of patterns you can successfully use within a room. Regardless of the style or amount of ornamentation, there should be an area in the room where your eye can rest. Use a solid color on an expanse of wall or carpet, or let the drapes or upholstery punctuate the room with solid blocks of color. If you are shy about combining bold patterns, save them for window or floor treatments, upholstery, and accents, rather than for walls.

Texture is another, subtler way to bring pattern and color to a room. Rattan furniture, upholstery with a deep, distinctive weave, fibrous wall coverings, embossed or coarsely woven drapes, and coir or cable-weave floor coverings all contribute a quiet rhythm of pattern and textured color. And this texture can be enhanced by light. Light plays upon textured surfaces and creates highlights and shadows; raised areas reflect light, and recessed areas trap shadows.

For a combination of patterns to be successful, as in this living room, there must be a consistent link between the colors or designs of the patterns. Here, rose or green tones appear in all the fabrics.

Light plays a key role in the color scheme of your living room. Here, well-placed lights bathe the room in a soft glow.

Photo: Kenneth Rice
Design: Jan Moyer Design, ASID

LIGHT AND COLOR

No single factor affects the color of your living room more than light. Light makes a reflective surface look lighter; glossy walls appear much lighter and brighter than matte walls of the same hue. Although dark colors recede and light colors move forward, a dark wall can be made to move forward—visually, that is—with the proper lighting directed on it.

Test colors under different lighting conditions. It is always best to select your colors under the same lighting you will use at home. A color looks paler in a sun-drenched room than it looks at night, of course. No amount of incandescent

lighting can make up for the absence of sun. Daylight flatters most colors. Incandescent lighting highlights yellow and red, but dulls blue and violet. Uncorrected fluorescent lighting has a decidedly blue cast. Color-corrected fluorescent lighting, which now is the standard, emits light that is almost identical to that of an incandescent lamp.

The exposure of the living room windows also affects color. Northern light is cool, with hints of green. Southern light is warm and pink. Western light is red orange. Eastern light, harsh with a yellowish hue, bleaches out the appearance of the colors it touches.

A SHORT HISTORY OF COLOR

Before the nineteenth century, when synthetic dyes were developed, there were limited choices of paint and fabric colors for living rooms. Paint pigments were natural and came from the earth. Fabric dyes were made primarily from plants and vegetables. The resulting palette, though serviceable, was muted: gray, red, green, brown, chalk white, terra-cotta, tan, and umber. The few brilliant, pure colors available were costly and derived from precious sources: gold, cobalt, ruby, and lapis lazuli.

In the nineteenth century, the drama of the decorative palette began to heighten. Brilliant synthetic dyes were produced and, as a result, a wider and more affordable range of colors transformed walls and furnishings. These new colors, such as bright pink, yellow, and magenta, seemed almost garish compared with the sturdy and somber earth- and vegetable-based colors.

In the 1920s, a brilliant white paint was developed that became the standard of sophistication and architectural purity. Stark white walls were a way to highlight the architecture of a room and make details stand out. Since the 1920s, a modernist aesthetic in the living room has meant white walls.

In the decades since the 1920s, many color preferences, such as the pale tints—safe and timid—of the 1950s, have emerged and declined. In the past decade, high color, especially on walls, has begun to challenge neutrals and tints.

Today, color is intense, vibrant, strong, and brilliant—more saturated than in previous decades. A raucous, eclectic blending of patterns, plaids, and wild colors has become a common sight in contemporary living rooms. The bright chrome green of the 1990s makes the pale green tint of the 1950s seem anemic.

Wall color is more expressive than ever. No one simply paints color on the wall anymore—surfaces are rag-rolled, stippled, glazed, combed, stenciled, and highlighted with trompe l'oeil motifs. These treatments are often complex, and the result is a many layered, rich patina of color and texture.

We are now more experimental about color combinations. Neutral doesn't have to mean the old standby gray, beige, white, or black. The classic neutrals are being challenged by the new neutrals. Today, a neutral is any color that blends well with the prevailing colors in a room. Maroon can be a neutral in a room of pink, blue, gray, and purple; deep olive can work as the neutral in a room of blue, black, and yellow.

Think of the wall as a blank canvas;
here, soft color is built up, complex,
and expressive.

The visual thread running through these connected rooms—the use of white and the architectural forms—links them, successfully unifying separate spaces.

Photo: Russell Abraham
Design: Swatt Architects

THE COLOR SCHEME

Almost any living room element can be a good starting point for planning a color scheme: a tiny repeating pattern in a treasured Oriental rug, a color in a comfortable checked sofa, a dominant hue in the painting you love but don't know how to integrate into the room, the rich gray stones of the fireplace, or even an armful of bright Thai silk pillows. Inspiration awaits you everywhere—floor, ceiling, furniture, window view. Start with a color you like, then build on it.

The living room is not a discrete room of the house, as bedrooms and bathrooms are, shut off behind closed doors. You will no doubt be able to see a hallway, an entrance, a staircase, or another room, from somewhere in the living room. Make the colors and styles of your living room harmonize with those of the surrounding rooms. If not, you will have a discordant room. There should be a clear link between spaces—a visual thread running through the connected rooms.

Decorating your living room is a bit like planning a garden: A well-designed garden will incorporate borrowed scenery. Your neighbor's perfect red maple will become—at least visually—your red maple if you plan the surrounding vegetation correctly. And so it is with the living room; there is a lot of scenery that can be borrowed. Glimpses of harmonious wall color and outstanding architectural elements of surrounding rooms will only enhance the design of your living room.

Harmonious walls and out-standing architectural elements of surrounding rooms enhance the design of this living room.

THE SCIENCE OF COLOR

Although your color scheme will ultimately be based on your visceral reactions to a certain color—ask fifty people to imagine red, and the chances are that no two will envision exactly the same hue—there is a science of color. Certain colors look well together, and others fight each other, because of their relative positions on the color wheel. Trust your natural response to color—but stop for a moment and read about the science of selecting harmonious colors. When you try to create a color scheme of more than a few colors, understanding the color wheel might help you to make wiser choices—color choices with which you can live happily.

THE COLOR WHEEL

In the seventeenth century, Sir Isaac Newton discovered that a ray of light passing through a prism reveals a rainbow, or continuous spectrum of color: red, orange, yellow, green, blue, indigo, violet. The color wheel, though somewhat abstract, represents in a circular format the linear spectrum that Newton saw. The wheel has three primary colors (red, blue, and yellow), three secondary colors made from combinations of the primary colors (orange, green, and violet), and the tertiary colors (for example, magenta and turquoise) made from mixtures of primary and secondary colors.

SOME COLOR TERMS

Color has its own vocabulary. *Hue* is the formal term for the color itself (for example, red). *Value*, or *tone*, is the relative lightness or darkness of a color. *Tints* are made by adding white to a color; *shades* are made by adding black. *Saturation* is the brightness of a color. *Temperature* refers to the perceived warmth or coolness of a color. For example, certain colors, such as red and yellow, are associated with heat and energy; these are warm colors; blue and green are cool colors.

Value Scale

Primary

Secondary

Tertiary

COLOR HARMONY

Colors can be combined in endless ways. But be careful that the colors you choose are not too close in tonal range—you may find that the difference between tones is too subtle to discern, especially in low-light situations. Here are five kinds of color schemes to explore. Perhaps you have already selected your colors, and they fit into one of these schemes.

A *monochromatic scheme* employs a variation of one color (for example, dark blue, medium blue, and light blue); or only white, black, and gray in combination.

Monochromatic

To create color harmony, use one of the two most basic kinds of color schemes: analogous or complementary. An *analogous color scheme* combines five or fewer colors, or their tints or shades, that are next to each other on the color wheel; for example, violet, violet blue, and blue. If you combine more than five colors that are adjacent on the color wheel, you will run into the field of the next primary color.

Analogous

A *complementary color scheme* is made up of colors from opposite sides of the color wheel, for example, violet and yellow, or red and green, or orange and blue. For maximum color contrast, place complementary colors side by side—they will seem to vibrate. Try red chairs against a green wall, or orange pillows on a royal blue sofa. Although two such colors will work well as the main colors in a room, you will need to augment the dominant scheme with other colors; otherwise the result will be too severe.

Complementary

Or try a *split-complementary scheme*, which pairs up the two colors next to a primary color with the color opposite the primary. For example, use yellow orange and yellow green, the colors adjacent to primary yellow, with violet, the color opposite yellow.

Split Complementary

A *triad color scheme* uses three colors, or their shades or tints, that are equidistant on the color wheel, such as blue, yellow, and red, or violet, orange, and green.

Triad

BEFORE YOU START

The living room has many functions. It provides a setting for entertaining, for curling up with a good book by a roaring fire or in a cozy reading nook, or for displaying an art collection. It serves as a guest room, a playroom for the kids, an informal dining room, even a home office. This multifunctional room can have equally as many moods. Before you start any redecorating, consider the functions and moods you want for the room. A vibrant exciting room—with a fiery palette? A soothing, restful place to recover from the day's trials—in fresh shades of light green or green blue? Or a room that will always be welcoming and happy—with sun-drenched yellow walls?

Find out before you go too far whether the colors you have in mind are the right ones for you. Surrounding colors influence the tone and vibrancy of a color. Place a clear red next to blue, then place the same red next to yellow. Your eye will be fooled—the red will look like two different reds. Remember that all colors are relative.

To test your ideas and the compatibility of colors and patterns, paste samples of fabric or paint swatches of color on white cardboard or large sheets of heavy paper. Start with your largest color area: the floor or wall. Next, on a smaller piece of cardboard or paper, paste drapery and upholstery samples. Then, on even smaller pieces, affix the details (fabric for pillows, dominant color in the art, and so on). Place these samples near a window and review them for several days, maybe a week. Do you still like them? Do you have the right order of color—is the biggest sample really the one you want to see the most of, or would it be more appropriate for the details? Taking a few days now to test your colors can prevent costly mistakes later.

Photo: Kenneth Rice
Design: Geoffrey De Sousa

The intense yellow walls of this cheerful, welcoming room glow from natural light and well-placed spotlights. The yellow tones, together with rich terra-cotta and blue, echo the colors in an intriguing collection of antiques and folk art.

A *living room full of neutral colors—without the distraction of bright hues—has subtle beauty, like a length of nubby tweed or a wooden bowl full of smooth river stones. Here, the lighter walls, window treatment, and ceiling emphasize the height and spaciousness of the room.*

CRISP NEUTRALS
Classic White, Beige, Black, and Gray

Neutrals run the gamut from light to dark and suggest the hues of nature: snow, clouds, chalk, sand, ivory, bamboo, oak, jute, stucco, rattan, corn husks, mushrooms, walnuts, marble, granite, slate, and obsidian. Neutrals are a mainstay in home decorating, classics that will never be outdated.

Today, neutrals are more popular than ever because of expanded interest in natural fibers—cotton, silk, muslin, linen—and undyed fabrics. Living rooms with soft, bleached, and weathered colors are appealing and inviting, like a summer day at the beach.

In the absence of bold color, other aspects of interior design take the lead, especially shape and texture. In neutral schemes where color has taken a back seat, the architecture and forms of the room are emphasized.

A neutral color scheme can be dramatically monochromatic—for example, black, gray, and white—or full of soft, diverse colors, such as bluish white, buttery beige, pink beige, tan, taupe, ivory, warm violet gray, and bleached or light wood. Because they are similar in tones, these hues will unify the room and direct the eye toward the myriad textures and forms.

All colors look well against walls that are painted white or off-white, the most prevalent neutrals. A white or off-white room will stay cool, calm, stark, and bright, day and night. However, white walls can be harsh and unforgiving of the quirks of a room.

CRISP NEUTRALS PALETTE

Neutrals do not have to be cool: yellow cream, beige, and rosy gray tones are warm. Enhance stark blue-white upholstery or fabric by placing a warm beige or gray close to it. Or tint white wall paint with some pink to make a room warmer and more inviting. But if you like the modern, sophisticated atmosphere of a cool room—perfect for showcasing art—choose white with a tint of green or blue.

Bright White

Linen White

Fawn

Cashmere

Metal Black

Linen Tan

Here, the carpeting, upholstery, and walls are similar in hue and tone. The designer uses gray, tan, and brown accessories to add subtle, essential contrast, definition, and rhythm to the soft, monotone scheme.

Soft Ebony

Pale Desert

Deep Petal

Linen White

With its restricted palette—linen white, beige, gray, black, coral pink, and gold—and its folding screen, silk pillows, and spare lines, this room marries design elements from the East and West.

Photo: Russell Abraham
Design: Kay Heizman, ASID

Design: Roche-Bobois

Cashmere

Metal Black

Medium Spiced
Pumpkin

In this nearly monotone setting, the furnishings and forms of the room take precedence. The architecture, the folk-art themes of the pillows, and the textures of the upholstery and accessories serve as points of interest.

Deep Flax

Bleached
Wood

Linen White

Coral Tan

*Rather than compete
with a spectacular
view, this interior
complements and
frames it. The soft
neutral colors—the
mustardy tan, white
hues, creamy beige,
and bleached
wood—are accented
with glistening gold
accessories.*

Photo: Steve Vierra
Design: Jessica Flynn

Photo: Kenneth Rice
Design: Guy Chaddock

Medium Parchment

Soft Cayenne

Lemon Meringue

The rich built-up color of the rubbed walls holds the room together elegantly and reflects the warm yellow tones of the wood, chair, and tiled floor.

Custard Yellow

Melon Gold

Silk Red

Medium Lily

Use direct incandescent lighting to bring out the yellow tones in a room. Here, the shelf lighting intensifies the yellow of the wood as well as the pale but sunny tint of the wall.

Photo: Russell Abraham
Design: Jan Gardner Design

Photo: Kenneth Rice
Design: Thomas Bartlett

Desert Dawn

Marble Green

Light Mandarin Ice

Deep Black Slate

Art does not have to be mounted on white walls only. In this room, there is a satisfying relationship between the wall color, with a mottled greenish tint, and the palette of the painting and framed calligraphy.

Bright White

Pale Tiger Lily

Dark Black

Bright white and light-filled interiors are airy and spacious; contrasting details stand out boldly. In this sleek design, the black accents and golden highlights anchor the whiteness and add a sense of rhythm.

Photo: Douglas Johnson
Design: J. Hettinger Interiors

Photo: Kenneth Rice

Tan Bamboo

Pale Auburn

Honey Brown

The warm glow of the fire brings out the rosy tones of the furnishings and walls. The earthy palette perfectly suits the architecture of this compelling space. Bright light would bleach out the subtle wall color.

Pink Bamboo

Meadow
Green

Dark
Chocolate

*The pink-beige tones
of the walls, carpet,
window treatments,
brocade chair, and
striped upholstery
are nearly identical;
this similarity of
pleasing colors uni-
fies the design.*

Photo: Russell Abraham
Design: Ron Martino, ASID

Photo: Russell Abraham
Design: Bob Rogers, ASID

Desert Sand

Alabaster Stone

Light Pecan

The subtle gray plays a key role in balancing this mostly beige color scheme. Look closely and you will see gray everywhere: in the fireplace marble, drab green walls, woven pillows, and beige of the carpet.

Coffee Mocha

Rich White

Bright White

Bricks are a prominent textural element, even when painted. The texture of the bricks dominates this white and soft brown room. The shadow trapped between the bricks empha- sizes the pattern and rough geometry of the wall.

Photo: Kenneth Rice
Design: Ann Saavedra

Photo: Russell Abraham
Design: Nancy Staggs

Linen White

Deep Berry

Wild Iris

A panoramic view, such as this one, could overpower a white room. The rich color and lively geometry of the carpet help the room hold its own against a powerful landscape.

Photo: Russell Abraham
Design: Maxcy Design Associates

Linen Tan

Bright White

Orange

Bright Lichen

Metal Black

This cream and ivory interior is electrified by an unlikely yet successful combination of orange and green pillows. The black and white chairs, which define the sitting area, balance the energy and color intensity of the pillows.

Deep Black Slate

Linen Tan

Natural light brings out the subtle yellow of these neutral colors. The black details and intensely colored pillows and art punctuate the expanse of near monocolor and provide brilliant focal points.

Bright White

Whipped Butter

Photo: Russell Abraham
Design: Jean Crawford, ASID

Photo: Russell Abraham
Design: Jane Antonacci, ASID

Pale Blue Gray

Old Gold

Harvest Straw

Deep Black
Slate

The palette is controlled—all neutrals, no brights—yet the colors are intense, concentrated, and rich. The black, tan, brown, and glistening metallic tones speak of the earth and a poetry of form and texture.

Photo: Russell Abraham
Design: Kennedy/Lutz Architects

Pale Auburn

Pale Nutmeg

There is rhythm, and not just from the piano, in this dynamic interior. The stripes and rectangles in the architecture, floorboards, cupboards, tables, and chairs invigorate the space. The visual composition is powerful: controlled color and exquisite geometric form.

Coral Tan

Bright White

Beach Sand

Black Stone

Rich White

Dark Black

Photo: Kenneth Rice

The sophisticated palette of neutral tones—black, tan, beige, and white—unifies the room and its striking art collection. The dramatic lighting highlights the art and accentuates the depth of an unusually proportioned space.

Photo: Russell Abraham
Design: Swatt Architects

Light Neutral Gray

Forest Charcoal

Deep Cranberry

Medium Lichen

Window seating takes advantage of the enticing light and view. The loden and cranberry pillows echo the rosy tones of the carpet and the greenish tiles in this well-unified scheme of off-white, gray, and gray green.

Black Slate

Fawn

Deep Flint

Bronze

Photo: Russell Abraham
Design: Von Naeher Design

The patterns and textures of nature characterize this space. The flagstone floor and hearth inspired the range of neutrals that intermingle in this comforting retreat.

Rich violet walls, echoing the tones of the painting, make this room seem intimate. Surrounding a room with violet and mauve gives the cool sophistication of blue and the warmth of red.

ROMANTIC PASTELS
Soft, Dreamy Tints

Photo: Russell Abraham
Design: Design & Interiors

A pastel palette is gentle, soft, light, and romantic. A pastel is a tint of a certain hue that combines many parts white to one part color; the white keeps the color pale and soft. Unlike intense hues, pastels—because of their common white base—can be used in unlimited combinations.

Pastels accommodate a broad range of living room styles: from ornate and traditional to minimal and modern, and every style in between. For a pale but dramatic look, restrict your palette to one or two pastels; then use a full tonal range of each hue to enrich the room and create variation and color depth.

To give large rooms a more intimate feel, choose a warm, deep pastel like yellow or pink. It will make the ceiling seem lower and the walls closer, creating a cozy space. To make smaller rooms seem larger, use cool pastels like blue or green.

If you have cool white walls or a white ceiling in your pastel room, pale blue or green furnishings will intensify the coolness of the white. To warm up the room, use apricot or peach furnishings, which will provide a decidedly rosy glow to any nearby white.

ROMANTIC PALETTE

Pastels, in any combination and regardless of their position on the color wheel, mix well because of their common element: white. Pastels are sun-washed colors; a gentle weathering of a hue produces a tint. A palette of pastels, like an open window on a summer day, will make your living room airy, spacious, and fresh.

Pink Rose

Custard Yellow

Mandarin Ice

Soft Plum

Pale Ocean

Blue Sea

Photo: Russell Abraham
Design: Nancy Taylor

A roomful of soft and romantic hues is always pleasing and never boring if the tones are varied. Even in a monochromatic scheme, a well-selected variety of tints, from pale to intense, can run through the entire tonal range.

Pale Lagoon Blue

Pecan Malt

Pale Bluebonnet

Even soft color can add punch and excitement to a room. Here, the blue-green walls make an appealing, rich background for the nearly monochromatic furnishings.

Photo: Kenneth Rice
Design: Modular Living

Photo: Kenneth Rice
Design: Agnes Bourne, ASID

Pale Ocean

Light Neutral Gray

Pale Custard

Blackbird

To energize a room of soft hues, try adding spots of deep contrasting color. Here, the elegant chairs and pale palette are juxtaposed with the dark but vivid wall sculpture—a kind of visual poetry.

Photo: Russell Abraham
Design: Sharon Marston, ASID

Pale Butter

Pink Lilac

Soft Plum

Deep Mountain Blue

Faded earth tones, weathered colors, natural fibers and textures, and over-sized terra-cotta pots bring the out-doors in. The soft shades—most within a narrow tonal range—keep the eye from being overwhelmed in this sunny living room.

Smoke Pink

Cool Taupe

Bright White

Deep Heather

A clear, bright pink and white color scheme, though appropriate for a child's room, could be too sweet for a living room. Try a sophisticated shaded pink with muted accents. Here, dark blue accessories and cool gray drapes and carpeting offset and enrich the pink and white tones.

Photo: Russell Abraham
Design: Jean Brown

Photo: Steve Vierra
Design: Richard Fitzgerald

Whipped Butter

Lily Green

Blackbird

Almost Rose

Combine pastels with intense, dark color to create a room of lively contrasts. Here, the butter-colored walls and pastel upholstery are the perfect foil for the highly colored and patterned rug and dark wood furnishings.

Warm White

Soft Plum

Mint Julep

Artichoke

Your upholstery or carpet pattern can inspire a color scheme. Here, the striking violet drapes and mint-colored accents refer to the colors of the upholstery, giving the living room a sense of well-coordinated color.

Photo: Russell Abraham
Design: Robert Miller Design Group

Photo: Russell Abraham
Design: R & R Design

Pink Hint

Foam Green

Ivory

Bold furnishings, accessories, and colors can overpower the architecture of a room. Here, the soft tints of wall and upholstery color and the shapes of the furniture are counterpoints to the stately architecture.

Tones similar in value are quiet and comforting. Most of the tones in this room, including those of the wood, are close in value, but not close enough to blur the distinctions between them.

Coral

Mandarin Ice

Cream White

Photo: Russell Abraham
Design: Swatt Architects

Photo: Kenneth Rice
Design: Diane Hynes, ASID

Pink Frosting

Pale Sea Spray

Soft Desert

Sandstone Tint

For a traditional living room to be successful, it needs warmth, supplied here by the glowing valentine pink walls. Accents of bright white and the gentlest of greens keep this formal space light and airy.

Rose

Dark Rose

Agate Green

In a high-ceilinged room, a light wall may fade into shadow at the top. In this elegant space, a darker pink molding sharpens the line between wall and ceiling and emphasizes the graceful architectural detail.

Photo: Kenneth Rice
Design: Cathryn LeBlanc

Custard Yellow

Clay White

Gray Sand

Eraser Pink

Photo: Russell Abraham
Design: Samantha Cole, ASID

No color warms up a room better than yellow. The yellow-based palette—creamy yellow walls, champagne-colored upholstery, and bleached wood—makes this intimate, romantic room glow.

Photo: Kenneth Rice
Design: Pamela Farnsworth

Blue Sea

Pink Rose

Here is a classic color combination in a contemporary setting. The inviting pink and powder blue theme repeats in the furniture and the carpet. This timeless combination of warm and cool creates a friendly room.

Rose

Lily Green

Pale Sandstone

A small space with grand architectural details will respond well to soft colors. The sumptuous upholsteries, pleasing palette—creamy tan, coral rose, and pale green—and elegant window treatments define this intimate setting.

Photo: Russell Abraham
Design: Design & Interiors

Photo: Kenneth Rice
Design: Richard Kenarney

Gray Day

Lavender Pink

Soft Turf

Here, the pale gray-blue walls are an unlikely but appealing contrast for the pale mauve and olive upholstery. The secret of this successful combination is that most of the colors have been derived from blue.

Medium
Wood Stone

Rose Petal

Mountain Blue

Soft Emerald

Lemon Yellow

Nothing works as well as white walls, rattan furniture, and cotton stripes to make a room fresh and summery. The color scheme of this room, derived chiefly from the pillows, offers pleasing ice cream colors.

Photo: Kenneth Rice
Design: Karen Carroll

Cameo Pink

Pale Butter

Blue Smoke

A cozy colonial setting is invigorated by a stretch of pink wall. The somberness of the braided rug, an appropriate match for the room, is balanced by bright white trim and upholstery and the colorful wall.

Photo: Russell Abraham
Design: Barbara Jacobs, ASID

Photo: Russell Abraham

Ripe Plum

Light Plum

Lavender

Gray Flint

To keep a high-ceilinged room inti-mate, create a low point of visual focus. Here, the eye-catching carpet not only demands attention, but warms up the cool, light-filled room and defines the central seating area.

Living rooms with natural palettes often take their colors from stone, brick, tile, slate, or wood features. These materials from the earth can help determine a color scheme. Stone gray and wood brown hues are as perfectly matched in your living rooms as they are in nature.

WARM EARTH TONES
The Terra-cotta Range and Naturals

WARM EARTH TONES PALETTE

The colors of the earth are generally muted, softened by weathering: shades of chalk white, tan, terra-cotta, russet, ocher, umber, and gray. The most effective accent colors will not overpower the subtlety of the palette. Try brick red, coal black, quartz pink, or loden green accents to heighten the contrast.

 Terra-cotta

 Warm White

 Brown Scarlet

 Soft Amber

 Natural Wood

Black Stone

The natural palette—the rich colors of earth, wood, stone, quarry tile, and marble—has become popular in both traditional and contemporary settings. Earth tones in the living room bring in the comfort and familiarity of the outdoors. Muted earth tones are neutral and ideal accompaniments to an array of natural textures and surfaces: craggy rock, silky polished wood and metal, shiny terra-cotta pottery, and the complex weaves of sisal and coir rugs or rattan furniture.

The spectrum of earth colors ranges from the palest creamy beige to the most intense terra-cotta brown. In nature, these muted tones are occasionally accented by brilliant colors like robin's-egg blue or the orange yellow of autumn leaves. And, as in nature, most accent colors in a natural-toned living room will be muted, with only occasional flashes of brilliant, pure color.

Terra-cotta is the workhorse of a natural palette; it is almost impossible to design a living room in earth tones without using terra-cotta hues. And terra-cotta does not mean just brown; tones range from a pale orange pink to a deep, dark black brown, encompassing shades of rusty red and fiery orange along the way.

To focus on textures, use a restricted palette. Here, brown tones with white and deep green accents combine with rattan and faux animal prints to create a sumptuous room, enclosed by glowing coppery walls.

Redwood

Alabaster Stone

Warm White

Blue Vapor

Some terra-cotta tones are rich enough to dominate a room. The terra-cotta upholstery is the focal point in this room of pale stone tones.

Photo: Russell Abraham
Design: Robert Miller

Here, the pink sofa, orange rug, and pink-brown and pink-orange upholstery are all shades of terra-cotta. These earthy tones are combined smoothly and harmoniously.

Terra-cotta

Raspberry

Natural Wood

Blue Spruce

Photo: Russell Abraham
Design: Gayle Walter Holmes

Mahogany

Bright White

*Nature's art can be integrated smoothly—
and naturally—into an interior color
scheme of earth tones. Weathered and
twisted branches, twigs, feathers, antlers,
and an animal print punctuate a white
and red-brown interior.*

Design: Roche-Bobois

Photo: Russell Abraham
Design: Lisa Schworer

Glazed Watermelon

Cameo Pink

Bright White

North Wind

Combine white with subdued earth tones to create sophisticated, warm pastels. Here, shades and tints of terra-cotta and crisp white accents keep this room fresh, not somber.

Photo: Russell Abraham
Design: Kay Heizman, ASID

Salmon

Deep Petal

Night Bird

Monochromatic schemes are most appealing when there is a variance of pattern or texture. In this intimate seating arrangement, similar shades of terra-cotta orange appear in stripes, prints, and solids to shape a cohesive design.

Cranberry

Bright White

Caramel

This living room speaks of colonial influences: furniture, milk glass, quilts, and other accessories. With its rich red undertones, the deep brown of the wall suggests a log cabin, albeit a very elegant one.

Photo: Steve Vierra
Design: Judy McMurray

Soft Cayenne

Creamy Yellow

Navy Indigo

*If brown hues are
rich enough, they can
single-handedly daz-
zle a room. Here, a
sofa of luxurious
brown—with the
warmest undertones
of red and yellow—
is the vibrant focal
point of a high-
ceilinged living room.*

Design: Roche-Bobois

Photo: Kenneth Rice

Brown Rose

Feather White

Old Wine

Bayberry

Monochromatic color schemes can work in traditional as well as in contemporary spaces. This traditional living room is unified by a lightened terra-cotta color scheme and a glowing bright white ceiling.

Photo: Kenneth Rice
Design: Axiom Design
and Diana Treter

Butterscotch

Eraser Pink

Green Gold

Without proper lighting and appropriate color schemes, rooms with wood ceilings and walls can be overpowering and cavelike. In this cozy and beautifully lit space, the tones of the glowing wood are echoed by the furnishings.

Photo: Russell Abraham
Design: Michelle Pheasant, ASID

Soft Desert

Redwood Hint

Black Stone

If your room includes dominant wood and stone elements, the color scheme will come easily. Here the furnishings amplify the colors of the natural materials in the room, and provide an appropriate stage for the ocean.

Cloudy Agate

Soft Amber

Dark Black

Clay White

A subtle earth-toned palette—here gray green and off-white—is the perfect background for folk art, photography, and period architecture. The black and white stripes of the upholstery, and the gold tones of the hand-hewn table and carpet, invigorate this small but grand interior.

Design: Jim Stagi

Pale Amber

Milk Chocolate

Herb Green

Pale Nutmeg

Here the earth palette is subtle, but offers a full range of mellow hues— beige, white, tan, yellow, green, orange, and brown—in this cozy reading corner, a discrete space away from the main action.

Photo: Kenneth Rice
Design: Michael Vincent, ASID

Brown Scarlet

Tan Cashmere

Pale Tiger Lily

Deep Flame

Photo: Russell Abraham
Design: Kay Heizman, ASID

Take advantage of a light-drenched room by keeping the palette light. Though the rattan furniture and oak flooring are essentially the same hue, the color scheme is not monochromatic; it is enhanced by color from the accessories and carpets.

Do not underestimate the power of red. It can turn a small space into a glowing jewel, or a large space into a sumptuous, regal palace. But if you are shy about color, try red as an accent; it will still be powerful enough to warm your room.

A FIERY PALETTE
Red Hues Ablaze

R ed is hot, bright, passionate, romantic—and powerful. It is also an international color of warning; red signs say Danger and Stop. And a red living room also demands attention. In large doses, red can fill a space with warmth quicker than a roaring fire can, and, even in small doses, it can dominate a room.

Red has always been a luxurious, regal color. Until the development of synthetic dyes in the nineteenth century, red color for walls and fabric was derived mostly from costly and rare pigments from the earth. It was found in sophisticated interiors and was a symbol of conspicuous wealth. As soon as synthetic dyes were perfected, the popularity of the color—in households of any scale or income—was assured. The new manufactured color was clear, replacing the often cloudy or subdued pigments of the natural reds.

Red does not represent one hue, but rather a broad, fiery palette. From an earthy brownish red on one end of the spectrum to a clear orange at the other end, it encompasses a vast array of hues, including orange red, terra-cotta, crimson, scarlet, vermilion, cherry red, strawberry red, berry red, blue-tinged red, purplish red, and, most electric of all, clear, unmitigated red.

Photo: Kenneth Rice
Design: Benita McConnell

A FIERY PALETTE

Use red to create an unforgettable, energetic living room. For a fresh, cheerful interior, include equal parts of red and white. To create a room that seems to vibrate, add green, the opposite of red. Try bright blue and yellow with red for a happy primary color scheme; or pink and yellow for tropical harmony.

Grenadine Orange

Flame Red

Chinese Red

Glaze Red

Maple Red

Soft Berry

Even accents of red can dominate a room. Although this cool, contemporary art-filled interior is almost completely white, red is the color that a visitor will remember.

Photo: Russell Abraham
Design: Design Partners

Glaze Red

Bright White

Soft Berry

Night Bird

Photo: Russell Abraham
Design: Sandy & Babcock Architects

Old Red

Red can be held in check by large white areas in a room. Here, the white walls, along with the wood flooring, carpet geometry, and prominent art, gracefully balance the clear red tones.

Pecan White

Dark Honey

Red hues are difficult to match precisely. Though the walls and carpet are not an exact match, they are close enough to provide almost seamless large-color areas. The supporting palette of white, pink, silver, and black keeps individual elements from disappearing beneath the red.

Flame Red

Quicksilver

Bright White

Deep Black
Slate

A minimalist living room often needs a focal point and source of warmth to make it comfortable. The red furniture offers color, warmth, and elegant curves to contrast with the spare geometry of the space.

Photo: Russell Abraham
Design: Swatt & Stein Architects

Photo: Russell Abraham
Design: Gayle Walter Holmes

Linen White

Old Red

Powder Blue

A little red can go a long way. Aside from the warm white furnishings, there is only a bit of red and other colors. But the red shapes and hues are strong enough to energize this space.

Lipstick Red

Aluminum

Steel Gray

Primary Yellow

Red can wake up even gray. The deep gray walls and large graphic painting are the perfect balance for the vibrant clear red of the chair and wall sculpture.

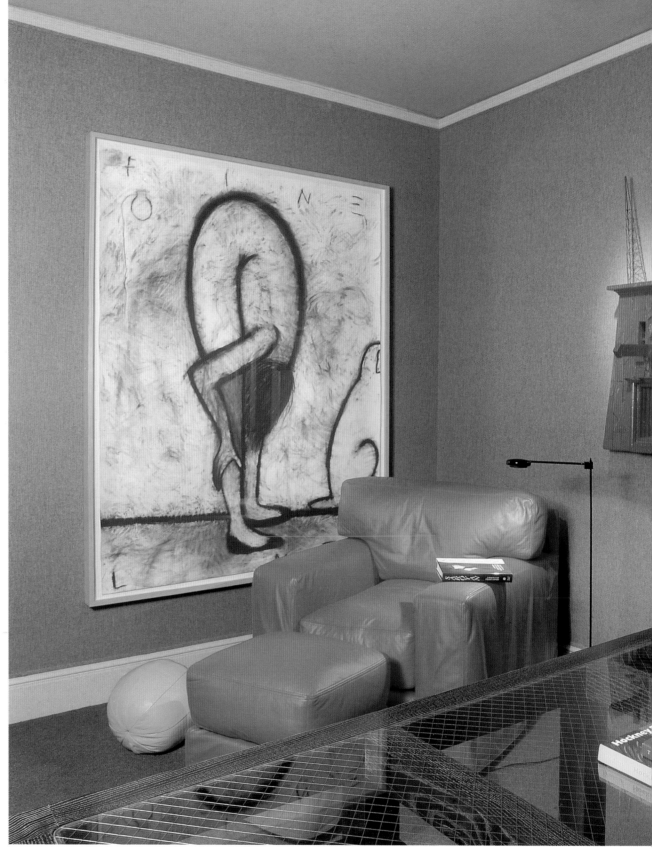

Photo: Kenneth Rice
Design: Agnes Bourne, ASID

Photo: Kenneth Rice

Deep Flame

Earth Brown

Mint Julep.

*Late afternoon sun, well-placed
lighting, or a roaring fire can intensify
the warmth and glow of red. The vel-
vety red chairs are ideally placed—
near the windows and fireplace—to
bask in the sources of light.*

Photo: Kenneth Rice
Design: Axiom Design
and Hermes Design

Chinese Red

Cameo Pink

Tan

*Red can be subdued and earthy like
redwood, brilliant and clear like ruby
or lacquer, or anywhere in between.
Here, two very different red tones
combine gracefully in a dramatic,
otherwise monochromatic, setting.*

Photo: Steve Vierra
Design: Claude Guidi

Grenadine Orange

Steel Gray

Conch Pink

For maximum contrast, place shades of red and green side by side. In this eclectic, comforting interior, the glowing red wall, with its striking orange overtones, complements and enlivens the rich green furnishings.

Folk art can be the inspiration for exotic color schemes. A color scheme that begins with a length of handwoven fabric or a rug, a painted wooden or clay mask, a highly decorated ritual vessel, a display piece of intricate clothing, or a wood-block print usually combines soft, natural color with vibrant accents.

EXOTIC RHYTHMS
Naturals and Brights Together

Photo: Russell Abraham
Design: Gayle Walter Holmes

The design of many living rooms begins with a prized collection of folk art, primitive art, handmade crafts, or handwoven rugs. These striking art objects can single-handedly inspire the color scheme of an entire room. The resulting palette is complex and full-bodied: naturals and brights combined.

These collected wares are often dominated by natural hues—pigments from the earth, subdued plant and vegetable dyes, and shades of terra-cotta—and resplendent accent colors. In your living room, as in the objects themselves, a natural combination of neutral soft hues with flashes of vibrant color can work well. This contrast of subtle and bold is distinctive and lends itself to a dramatic eclecticism.

In living rooms, handmade objects display a textural richness, a geometry of weave and pattern. Flashes of startling color add depth and vigor to the room. An exotic color scheme will be in harmony with nature, like a vivid wildflower on a sand dune, or a vibrant totem pole above a rocky cliff.

EXOTIC RHYTHMS PALETTE

There is surprise and quiet beauty in rooms where folk art, subdued natural colors, and saturated brights are combined. Brown and gray tones are natural foils for the flashes of bright yellow, red, blue, or green often found in folk art, handmade crafts, and objects from afar.

Soft Red

Night Shade

Leather Green

Stucco Gray

Deep Flax

Gold Pumpkin

Photo: Russell Abraham

East meets West in this sumptuous interior. The bronze sculptures, celadon pottery, luxurious red-brown leather chairs, intricate floral patterns, and bowl of taro leaves reflect a careful blending of styles and earth tones.

Metal Black

Bright White

Dark Flax

Bamboo

Soft Red

Night Shade

Old wood, rubbed smooth by generations of hands, gives a room a feeling of comfort. In this living room, the rich palette and sensuous textures are enhanced by beautiful hand-hewn wooden objects.

Photo: Russell Abraham
Design: Stephen Sanborn, A.I.A.

Design: Roche-Bobois

Leather Green

Wheat

Lipstick Red

Autumn colors—deep green, gold, and red—are as striking inside your house as they are outside. Well-worn metal vessels and a dramatic red elephant richly appoint this simple but intriguing space.

Photo: Russell Abraham
Design: RSA Interiors

Stucco Gray

Gold Pumpkin

Crimson

Crimson Brown

Red always jumps forward and demands your attention. Bright red accents, natural fibers, handmade objects from around the world, graceful architectural geometry, and an abundance of natural light all reflect a well-planned and cohesive design.

Forest Charcoal

Deep Flame

Pale Custard

Classic Blue

A room that contains art objects from many cultures does not need to look like a museum. The informal, accessible arrangement of the art objects and furnishings in this room enriches the small, appealing space.

Photo: Russell Abraham
Design: Kay Heizman, ASID

Soft Amber

Taupe

Brown Red

Maple Red

Black Slate

Gold Pumpkin

Wine Red

Julep Green

Rattan furniture gives any room a tropical atmosphere. Here, the theme is amplified by the plant, wall poster, and fabric that exemplifies an exotic palette: earth tones highlighted by different shades of bright red and green.

In this space, the blending of styles, rich rubbed wall treatment, striking primitive art, warm neutrals, hot reds, floral rug geometry, and plush fabric all combine in a smooth and cohesive eclecticism.

Photo: Russell Abraham
Design: Barry Johnson

Delft Blue

Pale Gold

Apricot
Orange

Tendril Green

Paprika

Like the sun in the sky, blue and yellow are a natural combination. Here, prints, patterns, and objects from around the world draw attention in an intimate space of warm and cool, sunny and subdued colors.

Photo: Steve Vierra
Design: Ann Sullivan

Flame Red

Carolina Sand

Black Stone

Corn Silk
Yellow

Driftwood
Gray

*In this modern, art-
filled space, where
the sky dominates the
ceiling and win-
dows, the muted
earth tones of the
sofas are enlivened
by the soaring red of
the chairs and the
bright primaries of
the sculptural table.*

Photo: Kenneth Rice
Design: Agnes Bourne, ASID

Although blue and green are both cool colors, they do not have to make a room cold. They bring a welcome sense of calmness and peace to their surroundings. With blue and green on your palette, you will be able to effortlessly create an endless range of moods.

SKY AND GRASS
Blue, Green, and Everything in Between

Blue and green are together everywhere in nature—just look at the horizon, where the sky meets rolling hills of green. And in your living room, too, these familiar colors, fresh from the outdoors, can be combined harmoniously in any ratio.

Rooms of most hues of green will be calming, restful, and tranquil—a breath of the outdoors. Dark green rooms speak of the sanctuary and comfort of the forest. Paler, softer greens are elegant and refreshing. Green (a combination of the primary colors blue and yellow) works well in color schemes of blue to violet as well as in those of yellow to orange.

Blue, like green, is peaceful, suggesting a calm sky or still water. Blue has an extensive range of hues: from deep violet to pale blue, from startling delphinium or cobalt blue to quiet, somber navy. Combine any hue of blue with orange, the opposite of blue, to create a dramatic, happy contrast—an energized color scheme. Or have red nearby to deepen the blue and create warmer tones.

Dramatic architecture, a well-placed skylight, and broad expanses of white make this living room airy and spacious. To keep the focus on the forms of the room, try a nearly monotone scheme; this elegant one doesn't compete with the architecture.

SKY AND GRASS PALETTE

Shades of blue and green bring tranquillity to a room. Add white and gray to this palette to make it sophisticated and modern. Add purple and red to warm it up. Certain green and blue hues work like neutrals—for example, navy blue and olive green. Combine these neutral shades with nearly any color to create different moods.

Cornflower

Flag Blue

Deep Iris

Teal

Pine Needle Green

Agate Green

Cornflower

Snow

Deep Iris

A limited palette—here, a few blue tones and crisp white—can provide richness and depth. The distinctive color scheme and billowing fabric are familiar and comforting, like blue and white delft.

Photo: Russell Abraham
Design: Glenna Cook, ASID

Photo: Douglas Johnson
Design: Sharon Moore

Bluebird

Putty White

Marigold

This living room elegantly combines a nearly monochromatic scheme with a riot of colors. The cool white tones of the walls, upholstery, carpeting, and lamps are nearly identical—an elegant stage for the bold, painterly print.

Wild Iris

Desert Sand

Flax

Bright Gold

This room—with its unforgettable purple-blue walls and golden baseboards and upholstery—has been turned into a walk-through jewel. The complex wall treatment includes a purple glaze, which intensifies and warms the deep blue undercoat.

Photo: Steve Vierra
Design: Roxy Grey, Marcia Connor

Photo: Russell Abraham
Design: RSA Interiors

Deep Mountain Blue

Soft Purple

Gray Denim

Here, the lavender of the pillows—only a bit of white away from pure purple—is the right intensity to form an appealing relationship with the soft blues, contributing to the coziness of the sitting area.

Sea Wind

Light Green Pea

Related colors create harmony. The main colors in this room, all adjacent on the color wheel—blue, blue green, green, green yellow, yellow—are harmonious here, as they are in nature.

Sunny Yellow

Photo: Kenneth Rice
Design: Benita McConnell

Pale Bluebonnet

Blue Smoke

Deep Iris

Soft Amber

Deep Black Slate

Photo: Russell Abraham
Design: David Meyers

Color can help define a quiet space away from the main action of the room. The regal stripes of the upholstery and the painted gold screen visually dominate the classically appointed setting.

Navy Blue

Pale Spruce

Pale Auburn

Red Brown

Photo: Russell Abraham
Design: Judith Tracy

Photo: Douglas Johnson
Design: Sharon Moore

Bright White

Blue Spruce

Contemporary interiors often incorporate minimal colors and forms. Here, a nearly geometric sofa is home to a palette of hyacinth and teal pillows. The color adds depth and a focal point to a mostly white room.

Hyacinth

Teal

The red tones of the light coral fabrics and mahogany table warm up this pleasing range of gray and midnight blue. The gold screen bounces light back in a warm glow to the center of the room.

Design: Roche-Bobois

Deep Flint

The pale, buttery walls set the stage for a dramatic, steely blue sofa. Because this simple room contains limited colors and decorative elements, the saturated color of the couch dominates.

Linen Yellow

Flag Blue

Lemon Meringue

Clear Crimson

Bright White

This reading corner offers bright primaries—or near primaries; the yellow is a few degrees away from a true primary. The soft yellow makes the color scheme quieter and more sophisticated than a bright yellow would.

Photo: Russell Abraham
Design: Nancy Taylor

Photo: Russell Abraham
Design: Joseph Bellomo, ASID

Dark Sky Blue

Adobe Brown

Except for the terra-cotta floor, the color in this room is quiet, held to a minimum so it does not compete with the architecture. The soft-blue tile wall unifies this spare interior.

Bright White

Hunter Green

Sunny White

Glaze Red

Pink Frosting

Large areas of white keep deep green walls from dominating a room. In this interior, the intense green is balanced by all the white and flashes of powerful red.

Photo: Douglas Johnson
Design: Kathy Monteiro

Pine Needle
Green

Mauve Red

Mauve Rose

Antique Brick

Complementary colors make a strong statement in these red chairs and pine green walls. The rich deep color of the chairs and the mauve print of the sofa work together because both colors contain blue.

Photo: Kenneth Rice
Design: Donna Gleckler, ASID

Photo: Russell Abraham
Design: Caryl Kurtzman, ASID

The mostly green palette here is easy on the eye and refreshing. The wall color—a pale tint of green, much more white than green—is reflected in the upholstery, plaid pillows, and glass shelves and tables. The white ceiling provides contrast for the walls and helps the palest green from disappearing.

Light Teal

Pale Spruce

Bright White

Photo: Russell Abraham
Design: Lois Lagonja, ASID

Green Gray

Medium Rose

Mandarin Ice

All greens blend well together, in the living room and in the garden. The green and pink chairs carry out the color theme of the sofa. Though the slightly yellow olive of the chairs corresponds closely to a green in the floral pattern, any green would do.

Agate Green

Pale Corn Silk

Quicksilver

Deep Desert

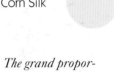
Tan Corn Silk

The grand proportions of this living room take on an easy formality in tones of olive. The white ceiling and soft yellow walls focus your attention— much more than dark colors would— on the stately architecture.

Photo: Russell Abraham
Design: Mehus Construction

Pewter

Desert

Dark Desert

Pale Desert

Olive and many shades of gray green can be considered neutrals because they combine well with most colors. Here, the green and support palette of gold and brown are just the right intensity to allow the elegant wood details to take center stage.

Photo: Kenneth Rice
Design: Ginne Kelsey, ASID, and Bob Rogers, ASID

Grayed Green

Desert

Pale Sandstone

Medium Delft

Photo: Steve Vierra
Design: Marian Glasgow

The rich, soft green of the walls appears to have spilled over from the palette of the painting. The match of the wall to the dry-grass colors of the art unifies this small but glowing space.

Although certain colors are rarely seen together in living rooms, almost any color will work in combination with any other color, if the relative elements of hue, tone, and tint are balanced.

UNEXPECTED COMBINATIONS
Soaring Surprises

We don't expect to see startling or eye-dazzling color in living rooms. Anything goes in product packaging and advertising, but we are hesitant about using boldly colored, vigorous patterns, undiluted primaries, or unconventional color combinations—for example, lime green and hot pink, turquoise and magenta, purple and orange—in our living rooms.

Color schemes with little contrast between colors are also surprising; for example, burgundy and deep red, deep navy and black, or a soft blue and soft green of the same tone. Without direct illumination, colors too close in value can disappear or merge at the flick of a light switch. And very pale colors—evanescent tints—can vaporize before our eyes when the sun sets.

Yet, an off-the-beaten-path palette may be just right for your living room. With professionally illuminated spaces, colors close in tonal range, or very pale tints, can hold their hue and infuse the space. To begin to appreciate vigorous colors, just keep looking at them. It is the unfamiliar that often puts us off. When a color scheme becomes familiar, it also loses its shock appeal; you grow comfortable with it and see beauty in its eccentricity. Under the right circumstances, even the most unexpected juxtapositions of color can succeed and charm.

UNEXPECTED COMBINATIONS PALETTE

In this palette, almost anything goes. The end result should be distinctive and quirky, maybe even break a few rules. Try navy with black, violet with rose, vibrantly colored bold patterns, or some screaming primaries to enliven a quiet space. Let your room surprise, startle, and delight visitors.

- Bright Gold
- Blue Periwinkle
- Creamy Orange
- Icy Blue Green
- Clear Purple
- Dark Rose

A common color component can link many colors that seem unrelated. In this unusual, striking room, that commonalty is red—it unifies shades and tints of peach, deep burgundy, clear pink, and pink tan.

Photo: Russell Abraham
Design: Madalyn Baker, ASID

Soft Aqua

When colors are soft, it is easier to bring them together in unlikely combinations. Here, the apricot sofa is an elegant counterpoint to the combination of pale aqua and olive.

Icy Blue Green

Shell Coral

Medium Leaf

Photo: Russell Abraham
Design: Von Naeher Design

Lilac Pink

River Blue

Blue Periwinkle

Creamy Orange

Sumptuous materials can soften strong contrasts. The complex blue green of the thick carpeting and a deeply woven throw are a fine juxtaposition to the silky mauve sofa; the pale periwinkle walls and flashes of orange are bold additions to an eccentric, but successful color scheme.

Photo: Russell Abraham
Design: Swatt Architects

Clear Purple

Carnelian

Primary Yellow

If given enough space, vibrant, saturated color can work with any design style. This brilliant combination of purple, red, and yellow dominates an airy, uncluttered contemporary room.

Black Slate

Deep Desert

Blue
Bandanna

Auburn

*Black walls and
gold ceilings are
rarely seen in homes
because they can
overpower most inte-
riors. Yet, here, a
skillful and intrigu-
ing blending of color,
disparate objects,
and pattern creates
a well-balanced,
friendly space.*

Photo: Kenneth Rice
Design: Diana Treter

Photo: Kenneth Rice
Design: M. J. Sammann

Custard Yellow

Bright Gold

Dark Rose

Green Gray

Yellow walls make a room sunny and bright. The deep yellow walls and ceiling complement the architecture. Elaborate drapes and heavy ornamentation are showcased beautifully in this unlikely palette of rose, yellow, drab green, and black and white.

Salmon

Storm Cloud

Wood Stone

Cameo Pink

Muted Olive

Here, soft, harmonious colors—a balance of warm and cool—unify the art, architecture, and forms. A broad, muted palette brings together a quirky, zestful living room designed for art, discussion, and comfort.

Photo: Kenneth Rice
Design: Lou Ann Bauer, ASID

Photo: Kenneth Rice
Design: Agnes Bourne

COLOR SWATCHES

HOW TO USE THE COLOR SWATCHES

The color swatches here represent the individual palettes of each of the living rooms in this book. The colors are arranged in color-wheel, or rainbow, order. Browse through these and when you find a color that you like and want to use, turn to the page listed for an example of a palette that includes that color.